CW00751854

Church Linen, Vestments and Textiles

Church Linen, Vestments and Textiles

Margery Roberts

Illustrations by
Nicholas Elder

Published in association with
THE SOCIETY OF THE FAITH

Copyright in this volume © The Society of the Faith, 2015

First published in 2015 by the Canterbury Press Norwich
Editorial office
3rd Floor, Invicta House,
108–114 Golden Lane,
London EC1Y 0TG

Canterbury Press is an imprint of Hymns Ancient & Modern Ltd
(a registered charity)
13A Hellesdon Park Road, Norwich,
Norfolk NR6 5DR, UK

www.canterburypress.co.uk

All rights reserved. No part of this publication may be
reproduced, stored in a retrieval system, or transmitted,
in any form or by any means, electronic, mechanical,
photocopying or otherwise, without the prior permission of
the publisher, Canterbury Press.

The Author has asserted her right under the Copyright,
Designs and Patents Act, 1988,
to be identified as the Author of this Work

British Library Cataloguing in Publication data

A catalogue record for this book is available
from the British Library

978 1 84825 740 5

Typeset by Regent Typesetting
Printed and bound in Great Britain by
CPI Group (UK) Ltd, Croydon

Contents

[v]

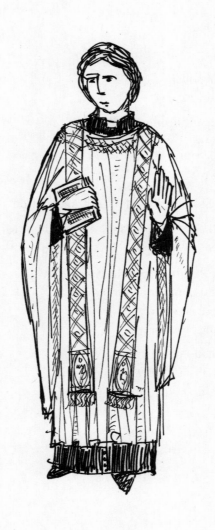

The Society of the Faith

The Society of the Faith is a small charity founded in 1905 by two high-churchmen, the Reverend Canon J. A. Douglas, Vicar of St Luke's Camberwell, and his brother, the Reverend C. E. Douglas.

The Douglas brothers were committed to the catholic tradition within the Church of England. The Society they founded was to be 'an Association of Christians in communion with the See of Canterbury for mutual assistance in the work of Christ's Church and for the furtherance of such charitable undertakings as may from time to time be decided upon, more especially for the popularisation of the Catholic faith.'

The Society's first work was the printing of Sunday School stamps, which proved immensely popular. This success inspired the foundation of Faith Press, publishing books both scholarly and popular, as well as church music.

In 1916 the Society also founded Faith Craft to produce high-quality vestments and church furnishings. Their biggest single commission was the complete refurbishment of St Mary-le-Bow in London after the Second World War.

The Douglas brothers lived on into the 1950s. Times (and tastes) were beginning to change, and this eventually led to the closure of both Faith Press and Faith Craft in 1973. However, The Society of the Faith remains committed to its original objectives: seeking to promote good standards in publishing and church furnishing, and in theological education.

Recent co-publications in association with the Canterbury Press include Michael Yelton's *Anglican Papalism* (2005), Paula Gooder's *The Meaning is in the Waiting* (2008), and John Gunstone's *Lift High the Cross: Anglo-Catholics and the Congress Movement* (2010). In 2013, in association with Church House Publishing, the Society brought out Canon Robert Reiss's book *The Testing of Vocation: 100 years of ministry selection in the Church of England*.

Since 1935 the Society has held the lease of Faith House, 7 Tufton Street, Westminster. Faith House is currently home to the church furnishers Watts & Company, the National Churches Trust, Sion College and Open Europe.

Foreword

by the Bishop of Southwark

The care of church linen and vestments is an important service, yet one that is often unnoticed, save by the priest and those serving at the altar of God. On the riverside of Southwark Cathedral stands the Livery Hall that is the home of the Worshipful Company of Launderers. By the standards of the City of London, it is a rather new Company, but the Launderers flourish under a motto that is far older: 'Cleanliness is next to Godliness'. It is a phrase that resonates with a powerful familiarity and asserts a timeless truth on which many generations have been raised.

If indeed cleanliness is next to godliness then how vital it is that proper care is taken of those things we place under, around or near holy things. These include the vestments that we wear as well as such everyday items as cassocks, surplices and albs. On my first day in residence at Theological College, the Principal addressed the new intake and exhorted us 'never to become overfamiliar with holy things'. Our care for the things of God needs to be reverent and prayerful, offered with gladness and joy. It is good to have a high doctrine of such things, for the quality of the care we take to prepare well for the Ministry of Word and Sacrament sets the standard and makes visible our priorities. Linen and vestments that are well cared for speak of our attentiveness to holy things as part of our offering of worship and praise to Almighty God.

I am grateful to Margery Roberts and The Society of the Faith for the issue of this helpful book which contains much practical wisdom and advice, together with cheerful drawings by Fr Nicholas Elder, Vicar of St George's Camberwell in the Diocese of Southwark. I commend it to you as a valuable resource in sacristies and vestries throughout the Church, whatever the parish tradition might be, in particular to those who undertake the quiet ministry of ensuring the good order of church linen and vestments.

+Christopher Southwark

Introduction

In 1932, the Faith Press published a booklet called *Altar Linen: its care and use* by Warren Richards. This useful publication was revised and reprinted several times before the Faith Press was wound up in the 1970s by its parent body, The Society of the Faith.

Although copies of the booklet still lurk in church vestries around the country, it has become apparent that there is now a substantial demand for a completely new practical guide, not only to the care of church linen, but also to the use and care of vestments. In the 80 years since the original booklet was produced, there have been notable changes in liturgy and styles of worship; but, in my experience of the Church of England as administrator, churchwarden, acolyte and subdeacon, I have not come across a parish that does not use at least some linen and textiles in its services or does not expect high standards of neatness and cleanliness.

This short guide gives advice about how to wash, starch, fold or otherwise care for the main items used at the altar, as well as briefly describing their use. The original format has been expanded to include information about vestments and garments, plus detailed advice about cleaning and storage. Although I have, in the interests of clarity and uniformity, used expressions or descriptions that might be identified with certain church traditions (for example, 'altar' instead of 'Holy Table'), my hope is that all parishes will find the guidance helpful, straightforward and eirenical. Space has been left on the pages of text for users' own notes.

Warmest thanks are due to the Bishop of Southwark, the Right Reverend Christopher Chessun, for his encouraging foreword, and to the Reverend Nicholas Elder for his excellent drawings. Of those who have contributed suggestions and comments, I must particularly thank Dr Arthur Waters for checking my science and the directors and staff of Watts and Company Ltd for their expert knowledge of linen and vestments.

Margery Roberts
The Society of the Faith (Incorporated)
Faith House
Westminster

Cloths and Covers

Introduction to Cloths and Covers

In Part One, all the main items of church linen and textile coverings are described briefly and illustrated, with advice provided about how they are used, cleaned, stored and repaired. The guidance is not intended to be definitive and there is space on the pages for users' own notes and memoranda. There is more detailed information about cleaning and storage in Parts Three and Four respectively. A short guide to liturgical colours is given as an Appendix.

The terminology may seem strange to those who are new to this field, but there is great practical sense in everybody calling the items by their accepted names. When I first became responsible for a sacristy, I was curious about the contents of some boxes that were piled up on a shelf. One, for example, had a tattered label bearing the words 'small square cloths'. This was not a bad term for corporals – which the box contained – but, when the minister standing at the altar whispers to someone to fetch a corporal, it is useful to have a box or drawer labelled accordingly.

One of the many glories of the Church of England is the great spectrum of traditions and convictions. For most parishes, some of the items described in this book will not be familiar at all. I have sometimes found, when assisting at the altar of my own rather traditional church, that a visiting priest has not known what to do with the burse and veil, because he or she has not handled them before. A more widespread knowledge of the textiles used in churches can only be beneficial, in that it removes some of the mystique without introducing (or encouraging) pedantry.

BURSE

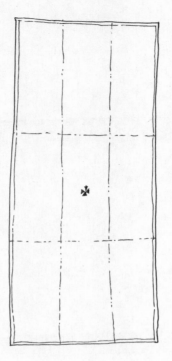

PURIFICATOR

[6]

Purificator

Use: used for wiping the communion vessels during the administration and after the ablutions.

Description: a rectangular or square towel, about 35 centimetres (14 inches) long, made of soft linen or cotton, hemmed. It may have a small cross or other emblem embroidered in white thread in one corner, in the centre of one side or in the middle.

Laundry: washed without starch; ironed folded in three, lengthways, and then in three crossways.

Storage: in a separate drawer, compartment or box in the sacristy or vestry, labelled so that it does not get mixed up with other items of linen. The area should be dry.

Repair: can be carefully mended, either by hand or machine, using cotton or linen thread.

Altar setting: the folded purificator is placed over the top of the chalice, with the paten above it. In some churches, the priest's wafer is placed on the paten, with the pall and silk veil on top of that.

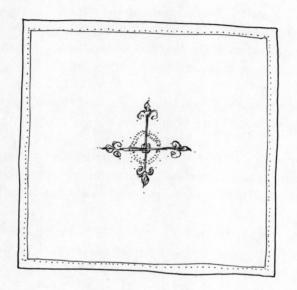

CHALICE PALL

Chalice pall

Use: used to cover the chalice and paten during the service.

Description: a white linen or cotton case or pocket, about 15 centimetres (6 inches) square, usually with a piece of white card inside to stiffen it. The top side of the case may be decorated with a cross. The underside may have an extra piece of linen lightly stitched on, which can be removed, if soiled, and replaced.

Laundry: the cover is washed and ironed, without starch. Remember to remove the card.

Storage: in a separate drawer, compartment or box in the sacristy or vestry, labelled so that it does not get mixed up with other items of linen. The area should be dry.

Repair: the card, if worn, can be replaced with new. The pall can be carefully repaired by hand or machine, using linen or cotton thread.

Altar setting: the pall is placed over the paten, and can also form a support for a chalice veil, if used.

Ironing a Corporal

imagine that the linen
square is divided into
9 smaller squares

1	2	3
4	5	6
7	8	9

Begin by folding squares 7-8-9
over squares 4-5-6

1	2	3
7	8	9

Next, fold squares 1-2-3
over squares 7-8-9

1	2	3

Now, fold square 1 over square 2

1	3

and then square 3 over square 1

3

Corporal

Use: placed on the altar under the communion vessels like a miniature tablecloth. In some traditions, a second corporal is used to spread over the vessels before consecration, instead of a silk veil.

Description: a linen cloth, about 50 centimetres (20 inches) square, hemmed and often with a cross embroidered close to the hem in the centre of one side.

Laundry: washed, with light starching, and ironed damp. It is folded as follows: first place it flat on the ironing board, best side up, and with the raised hems on the underside, with the embroidered cross facing you. Fold into three sections by turning the front section away from you and then bringing the back section forward on top of the front section. Next, do the same with the sides, first folding the left-hand section over the middle, and then bringing the right-hand side down on top, making a square. This method ensures that the best face is kept clean and that the cross ends up in the right position on the altar.

Storage: in a separate drawer, compartment or box in the sacristy or vestry, labelled, as with other items of altar linen. The area should be dry.

Repair: small snags or tears can be carefully mended, by hand or machine, using good-quality linen or cotton thread, as appropriate. However, shabby or stained corporals should be replaced with new.

Altar setting: the corporal is placed on the altar, with the cross facing the celebrant, under the chalice. Where a burse and veil are used, the corporal is kept, folded, in the burse when it is not spread on the altar. The burse opens like a book, with the spine on the left-hand side.

Lavabo towel

Use: used for drying the priest's hands after he or she has washed them before the eucharistic prayer.

Description: a white rectangular cloth, made of soft, absorbent cotton or linen (sometimes known as huckaback), up to 60 centimetres (24 inches) long and 30 centimetres (12 inches) wide, hemmed or fringed, and possibly embroidered with a white cross or other motif.

Laundry: washed without starch; ironed and folded in half, and then either into two or three sections, lengthways.

Storage: in a separate drawer, compartment or box, labelled. The area should be dry.

Repair: can be carefully mended or patched, by hand or machine, using cotton or linen thread.

Altar setting: placed on the credence table with the lavabo dish and jug. In use, when being offered to the celebrant, the towel is not completely unfolded but left as a long, narrow strip of more than one thickness.

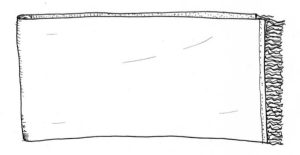

BURSE

Burse

Use: used in some churches to carry the folded corporal when not in use.

(The word is from the Latin *bursa* = purse.)

Description: a case made in the form of two conjoined envelopes, each containing card to stiffen it, about 23 centimetres (9 inches) square and hinged with stitching on one or two sides. The outside faces are covered in silk or other rich fabric, in a liturgical colour to match the veil (depending on the season) and often embroidered and decorated. The inside surfaces are made of linen or another fabric.

Laundry: not usually washed. Can be carefully dry-cleaned when the card is removed.

Storage: in a drawer or compartment in a vestment chest, with vestments of the same liturgical colour.

Repair: trailing threads can be carefully stitched back by hand, using thread of the same colour and type. More substantial damage may need to be repaired profession-ally.

Altar setting: before the service, it can either be propped up on the altar or placed over the veil on the chalice, with the spine on the left-hand side, so that the burse opens like a book. After communion, the priest usually folds up the corporal and replaces it in the burse.

VESTED CHALICE

Veil

Use: used in some churches for covering the chalice, paten and pall, before and after the consecration.

Description: a lined cloth, about 56 centimetres (22 inches) square, in the liturgical colour of the season, made of silk or other rich fabric and usually with an embroidered cross in the centre of one side, near the edge.

Laundry: if made of silk, not washed. Other fabrics may be washable. Silk veils are usually suitable for dry-cleaning.

Storage: in a drawer or compartment of a vestment chest, with vestments of the same liturgical colour.

Repair: loose threads can be stitched back carefully, using thread of the same colour and type. More substantial damage may need to be repaired professionally.

Altar setting: before the service, it is placed over the chalice, purificator, paten and pall, either tent-style or with the side away from the congregation turned up and laid back on top with the lining showing. If there is a cross on one side, this should face the congregation.

Altar frontal, frontlet and frontlet cloth

Use: used to cover and decorate the altar.

Description: the frontal is a cloth of silk or other rich material in a liturgical colour, often embroidered or otherwise decorated, 'tailored' to the size of the altar. The frontlet, also known as a super-frontal, is an ornamental band, about 15 centimetres (6 inches) deep, either in the same material as the frontal or in a contrasting one, which runs along the top of the frontal.

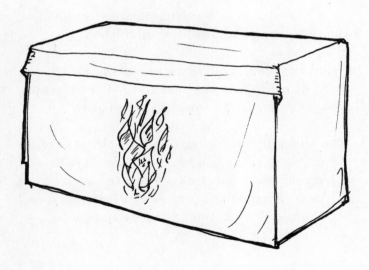

Laundry: the frontal and frontlet are not normally washed. Specialist dry-cleaning is needed. There are some 'fitted' cloths on the market which are made of viscose and polyester and these are washable. The frontlet cloth is made of thick linen or coarse cotton and can be unstitched from the frontal/frontlet, washed and ironed without starch.

Storage: can be folded and stored carefully in a deep drawer, with acid-free tissue paper between the folds. The best way to store frontals is in a top-opening chest, with the frontals suspended on rods which fit in sockets at each end, rather like files in a traditional filing cabinet.

Repair: old or fragile frontals need to be repaired professionally, unless the damage is very minor and suitable for careful mending by hand. Frontals and frontlets tend to wear thin along the front edge of the altar, either because of the hard edge behind or the priest's 'tummy rub' in front. This can result in an expensive repair.

Altar setting: usually left on the altar but changed to suit the season or occasion. There is normally an altar cloth (fair linen cloth) over the top and sides and, when no services are taking place, a dust cover as well. The flat type of frontal is often hung from a rod of non-ferrous metal supported by hooks under the top of the altar.

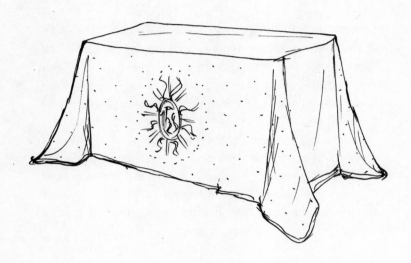

LAUDIAN FRONTAL

Altar pall, also known as Laudian frontal

Use: to cover most, or all, of the altar, depending on the type.

Description: a large cloth of silk or other rich material in a liturgical colour, often embroidered or otherwise decorated, sometimes with a fringe along the bottom, which is 'thrown over' the altar. The embroidery or other decoration faces the congregation.

Laundry: usually needs dry-cleaning, but there are some on the market that can safely be washed.

Storage: can be folded carefully and stored in a deep drawer, with acid-free tissue paper between the folds. If they are hung over rollers, they should be kept out of direct sunlight and, ideally, covered in cotton covers.

Repair: minor damage can often be carefully repaired by hand, especially if it does not involve any embroidery or other decorative work. Otherwise, professional expertise may be needed.

Altar setting: as with frontals, the pall is usually left on the altar for the duration of the liturgical season or feast indicated by the colour. There is normally an altar cloth (fair linen cloth) over the top and sides and, when no services are taking place, a dust cover as well.

Altar cloth and dust cover

Use: the altar cloth, often known as the fair linen cloth, covers the top of the altar and usually hangs down on each side, almost to the floor. The dust cover – also known as a 'day cloth' – is very slightly larger than the altar cloth and is used to cover it and keep it clean when not in use.

Description: the altar cloth is a long white cloth, usually of good-quality linen, the same width as the altar top and long enough almost to reach the floor on each side. There are usually embroidered white crosses to show the angles of the altar. The dust cover is very slightly larger than the altar cloth, made of a coarser material, white or coloured.

Laundry: both the altar cloth and the dust cover are washed, without starch, and ironed damp. The altar cloth, in particular, should not be creased or folded. This does present difficulties where the person doing the laundering lives some distance from the church, and the traditional advice is to wind the cloth on a roller. Cardboard rollers or tubes and acid-free tissue paper are excellent for transporting altar and credence table cloths, frontals and other items that should not be creased. Many churches keep an iron and ironing board in the vestry in order to help solve the difficulty.

Storage: the fair linen cloth should be stored wound round a roller in a clean, dry cupboard or drawer in the sacristy or vestry. If this is not possible, it should be folded, interleaved with acid-free tissue paper, and kept in a drawer. Creases need to be ironed out before use. The dust cover can be kept in a drawer or cupboard, folded neatly.

Repair: both cloths can be carefully mended by hand or machine, using good-quality linen or cotton thread.

Altar setting: the altar cloth is spread on the top of the altar, with the sides hanging down equally on both sides. The dust cover is placed over this when there is no service taking place.

CREDENCE TABLE

Credence table cloth

Use: to cover the credence table, shelf or cupboard.

Description: a white cloth, often made of good-quality linen or cotton, large enough to cover the top of the credence table/shelf/cupboard and hang down well at the sides. It may be embroidered and/or have lace around the edge.

Laundry: washed, without starch, and ironed damp. There should be no folds or creases.

Storage: folded carefully in a clean, dry cupboard or drawer in the sacristy or vestry. Creases should be ironed out before the cloth is used.

Repair: small tears and snags can be mended by hand or machine, using good-quality linen or cotton thread. Damage to lace, especially if it is old or fragile, may need a professional repair.

Setting: placed over the credence table/shelf/cupboard to act as a tablecloth for the cruets, wafer box, lavabo dish, jug and towel.

Pulpit with Fall

Pulpit fall and lectern fall

Use: to decorate the pulpit and lectern respectively. Apart from giving greater reverence to the liturgy of the word, pulpit and lectern falls allow a little of the liturgical colour into the nave, showing that it is not completely separate from the sanctuary.

Description: the pulpit fall is a square or rectangle of rich fabric, often in a liturgical colour and with decoration and a fringe on it, which hangs from the preacher's desk in the pulpit, facing the congregation. It may be attached to a stiff piece of card or board, covered in fabric, which goes over the top of the desk and supports the fall.

The lectern fall is very similar, although smaller, and fits on the lectern in such a way that the decorated side faces the congregation. Both the pulpit fall and the lectern fall can be made in almost any good-quality fabric and can be decorated in a wide variety of ways.

Laundry: this depends on the fabric and decoration, but most pulpit and lectern falls need to be dry-cleaned.

Storage: in a labelled drawer or box, preferably flat. When the falls are in liturgical colours, they can be kept in a vestment chest with vestments and items of the same colours.

Repair: minor damage, such as undone seams or trailing threads, can usually be put right with careful hand-sewing, using thread of the appropriate colour and type. More substantial damage, and particularly damage to old or delicate embroidery, needs professional attention.

Setting: both types of fall can be left in place if in a neutral colour or, when they match other hangings and vestments, changed according to the liturgical season.

PART TWO

Vestments and Garments

Introduction to Vestments and Garments

Part Two covers what clergy and others wear in church, including vestments used in some traditions for eucharistic worship. It includes both familiar, everyday items, such as cassocks and surplices, and episcopal garments, such as the rochet and chimere. The illustrations are likely to be as helpful as the text, if not more so. As with Part One, there is a description of each item, together with brief guidance about cleaning, storage and repair.

This is a practical guide, and not a book about liturgy or history. Consequently, I have made no attempt to enter into the sort of spirited (and occasionally heated) debates about the style or use of vestments that took place during the late nineteenth and twentieth centuries. Similarly, I have not, for instance, gone into detail about how exactly an amice is put on, or how a girdle is looped and knotted around the waist. I am more concerned with the recognition and care of the various items.

The range of fabrics used for both vestments and garments has widened considerably over the past 50 years and is likely to go on getting larger. This is to be welcomed because many of the newer synthetic or mixed-fibre fabrics are easier to care for and perhaps more affordable for financially challenged parishes than the naturally derived ones. However, for important occasions, high-quality materials and beautiful decoration are still appreciated.

CASSOCK & CINCTURE

Surplice & Stole

Cassock and cincture

Use: a cassock is a full-length, coat-style tunic worn by clergy, lay ministers, choir members, vergers and servers, as a basic garment under vestments, surplice, cotta or a gown. It can be worn as everyday dress by clergy. A cincture is a broad waistband or sash which goes over a cassock and can have long fringed ends known as falls.

Description: the cassock is an ankle-length fitted tunic with sleeves, generally black for parish clergy but sometimes with coloured piping in the case of canons, prebendaries, deans or archdeacons. Bishops may wear purple cassocks, and chaplains to the Queen and members of Royal foundations (such as Westminster Abbey) wear scarlet. Choir members often wear other colours. There are two main styles – the 'Sarum' style, which is double-breasted and fastens at the shoulders and waist, and the single-breasted style, with buttons down the front. The garment is supposed to be the descendant of the Roman tunic, worn under a toga, although the name derives from the Middle French *casaque*, meaning a long coat.

The cincture, usually in black, red or with piping, is either plain with a waist-fastening, or has long fringed falls. It comes in a variety of fabrics.

Laundry: this depends on the type of fabric used. Most moderately priced cassocks are made of polyester and can be washed in the washing-machine, following the usual washing instructions. However, cassocks can be made from a range of other fabrics, including pure wool, wool mixed with polyester, cotton mixed with polyester and viscose. In all cases, care should be taken to check the label or to consult the manufacturer. There are, for example, higher-priced polyester cassocks which should be dry-cleaned. The cincture should be washed or cleaned according to the fabric used.

Storage: cassocks usually on hangers in a clean, dry place. Cinctures should be stored in a labelled drawer or box.

Repair: undone seams and hems can be stitched up by hand or machine using thread of the appropriate type and colour. Tears and holes, if substantial, may need to be repaired professionally.

How worn: cassocks are worn over indoor clothing and, in the case of clergy, with a clerical collar. What is worn over a cassock depends on the wearer and the occasion. Clergy and readers/lay ministers, when conducting or participating in non-eucharistic services, can wear a surplice with scarf, academic hood and possibly bands, a form of dress known as choir dress or choir habit. For celebrating the Eucharist, clergy normally wear a surplice and stole or full vestments (alb, amice, stole and chasuble). Clergy can wear a cotta instead of a surplice. Altar servers can wear surplices, albs or cottas. Choir members can wear surplices or gowns. In all cases, the cassock is the basic item of ecclesiastical wear. The cincture fits round or slightly above the waist.

Cassock-alb

Use: a relatively modern garment which combines a cassock, alb and amice.

Description: a full-length, white or cream, cassock-like garment, available in a variety of fabrics from polyester to wool. There are various styles, some double-breasted, some single-breasted and some with hoods.

Laundry: this depends on the fabric used. Moderately priced ones are generally made of polyester and can be machine- or hand-washed. Cassock-albs made of other fabrics may require dry-cleaning.

Storage: on a hanger of the appropriate size, in a clean, dry place in the vestry.

Repair: as with cassocks, undone seams or hems can usually be stitched up by hand or machine, using appropriate thread. More extensive damage may need professional attention.

How worn: in place of cassock, alb and amice. Some styles are worn with a girdle.

ALB WITH AMICE AND GIRDLE

Alb, girdle and amice

Use: white garments worn by both clergy and laity for services, usually with vestments, depending on parish tradition.

Description: the alb is a full-length white robe, sometimes having a lace border. It is said to derive from the ancient Roman tunic (Latin *albus* = white).

The amice is a white rectangle of cloth, about 92 centimetres (36 inches) by 66 centimetres (26 inches), used as a neckcloth to protect the edge of the vestment, with long strings of tape attached to two corners (Latin *amictus* = wrapper). In some traditions, the amice has an apparel stitched or pinned to it. This is like a stand-up collar made of a rich fabric, co-ordinating with the vestment being worn. The alb and amice can be made of linen, cotton or polycotton.

The girdle is usually made of white, plaited cotton, but can be made of plaited rayon/viscose, often in liturgical colours. The ends are usually left unplaited and knotted to form fringes.

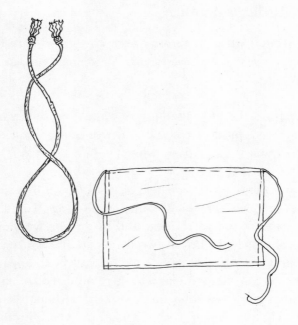

Laundry: the alb and amice can usually be washed, without starch, and ironed according to the advice for the fabric. Where there is an apparel, this should first be removed. The amice can be lightly folded to form a smaller rectangle for storing, with the strings tucked inside. Albs that have a lace border need to be washed with care, especially if the lace is old and precious, and ironed damp, although advice should be sought in advance if there is any doubt. The waist girdle, in white or a liturgical colour, can usually be washed and dried normally, without ironing.

Storage: albs are best kept on hangers of the correct size in a clean dry place in the vestry. Amices and girdles should be kept in labelled drawers or boxes.

Repair: undone seams and minor tears to albs and amices can be mended by hand or machine, using linen, cotton or polycotton thread, as appropriate. The tapes on amices can be replaced, using suitable cotton tape. Torn lace on albs may need to be repaired professionally.

How worn: the alb is worn over a cassock, with the girdle tied around the waist. The amice is used as a neckcloth with an alb and chasuble, dalmatic or tunicle, usually put on over the cassock, with the tapes tied at the back of the waist. Once the alb is put on, the amice is tucked in neatly around the neck. Some people prefer to wear a cassock-alb instead of three separate garments.

In the Roman Catholic Church, the girdle is usually known as a cincture and the cincture as a fascia.

SURPLICE   COTTA

Surplice and cotta

Use: white garments worn by both clergy and laity for services, according to parish tradition. The surplice forms part of choir dress or habit.

Description: the surplice is a white garment, reaching to below the knees, with full, loose sleeves. Its use dates from the Middle Ages, when clergy wore a linen gown over warm clothes (Latin *superpellicium* = over fur). The cotta is like a short surplice, with shorter sleeves and a square neck, and sometimes has a decorated border or lace edging. Both can be made of cotton, linen or polycotton.

Laundry: washed, without starch and ironed according to the advice for the fabric. Traditional surplices, made of fine cambric, do need to be starched lightly, as the fabric is otherwise limp. Care should be taken if the cotta has a lace border, especially if the lace is old or delicate. It may be possible to hand-wash it gently but, if there is any doubt, advice should be sought.

Storage: surplices and cottas can be stored on hangers of the right size in a clean, dry place in the vestry.

Repair: undone seams or hems can be mended by hand or machine using the appropriate thread. More extensive damage may need to be dealt with professionally, especially if it involves lace or a decorative border.

How worn: both the surplice and cotta are worn directly over a cassock. When worn as part of choir dress or habit, the surplice is worn with hood, scarf and often preaching bands.

GOTHIC CHASUBLE

Chasuble, stole and maniple

Use: the chasuble is worn at the Eucharist by the celebrant. The stole is worn at all sacramental services, including marriage. The maniple can also be worn at the Eucharist, although it has largely fallen out of use.

Description: the chasuble is a large vestment in a liturgical colour which goes on over the head and hangs down at the front and back. There are two main styles – the Gothic, which is oval and hangs in folds, and the baroque or Latin, which is cut away at the shoulders to form a rectangular shape at the back and a shape like a bass fiddle at the front. It can be made of almost any fabric, from silk brocade to tree bark, and there is usually some decoration on the front or back such as a band of orphreys (rich embroidery or decoration). The term chasuble is thought to derive from the Latin *casula*, meaning a little house, a reference to its size and shape.

The stole is a long band of material in a liturgical colour, of similar fabric to a chasuble, often embroidered or decorated and with fringed or plain ends. There are two main shapes – a straightforward band of even width, about 8 centimetres (3 inches) wide, and 'Sarum' style, with splayed ends. The stole is sometimes stitched to fit around the back of the neck, forming a wide angle with a cross embroidered at the centre. The maniple is like a small stole, doubled over and stitched loosely so that it can be slipped over the wrist.

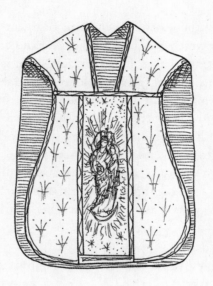

LATIN CHASUBLE

Laundry: this depends entirely on the type of fabric used. Most chasubles, stoles and maniples are not washable and should be professionally dry-cleaned. However, there are ones on the market in washable fabrics.

Storage: in a drawer in a vestment chest, carefully folded, with other items of the same liturgical colour. Storing chasubles on hangers is not recommended because, over time, the ends of the hangers can wear through the fabric. However, if there is no vestment chest, large hangers should be padded for use with vestments. Vestments should be kept out of direct sunlight.

Repair: minor damage, like trailing threads and undone seams, can be mended carefully by hand, using thread of the appropriate colour and type. More major damage should be dealt with professionally.

How worn: the chasuble is worn over a cassock, alb (with girdle), amice and stole, or over a cassock-alb, girdle and stole. The stole, when worn at the Eucharist, is worn over the alb or cassock-alb, either crossed over the chest and held in place by the girdle, or hanging straight down. When worn for other services, it is placed around the neck over the surplice or cotta, with the long ends hanging in front. For a deacon, it is worn diagonally over the left shoulder and secured at the right hip. The maniple is worn over the left wrist.

DALMATIC

Dalmatic and tunicle

Use: worn by the deacon and subdeacon respectively at a Solemn Eucharist (High Mass). The tunicle is also sometimes worn by the crucifer (cross-bearer) in processions.

Description: both vestments form part of a set with the chasuble, being usually made in the same fabric and in a liturgical colour. In shape, they are rather like a tabard with wide sleeves. They can be decorated in various ways, including having coloured cords at the shoulders, but the dalmatic usually has two horizontal bars of decoration, and the tunicle one. The term 'dalmatic' derives from Dalmatia (now part of Croatia), where the garment was originally worn by those of high rank. It became a liturgical vestment in the fourth century. The term 'tunicle' comes from the Latin *tunica*. The garment became a liturgical vestment in the ninth century.

Laundry: both should be cleaned in exactly the same way as the matching chasuble.

Storage: in a drawer in a vestment chest, carefully folded, with other items of the same liturgical colour. They should preferably not be stored on hangers, but if there is no chest, large hangers should be padded in order to minimize damage to the vestments.

Repair: minor damage, such as undone seams or hems, can usually be stitched by hand, using thread of the

TUNICLE

appropriate type and colour. More substantial damage may need to be dealt with professionally.

How worn: both vestments are put on over the head and are worn over a cassock, alb and amice or a cassock-alb. The deacon also wears a stole, diagonally, over the left shoulder and tied or secured at the right hip.

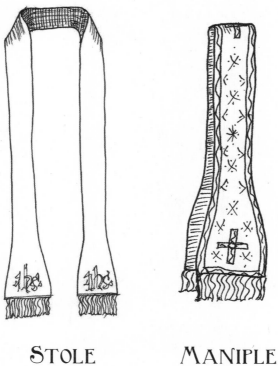

STOLE   MANIPLE

COPE (FRONT)

Cope

Use: worn by clergy (and certain laity, such as lay canons) for processions and special occasions, including weddings and funerals. Especially popular in cathedrals and Royal foundations.

Description: a large semi-circle of usually richly decorated material in a liturgical colour, worn as a cloak and fastened across the chest, usually by means of an ornamental clasp or tab known as a morse. At the back is a nominal hood, often a shield-shaped panel of rich embroidery or decoration. The term 'cope' comes from the Latin *cappa*, meaning a cloak with a hood. This is exactly what a cope was historically, when it was used only for outdoor processions.

Laundry: copes nearly always need to be professionally dry-cleaned.

Storage: a cope should ideally be stored in a vestment chest, carefully folded, and not on a hanger, as the ends of the hanger cause the fabric to become worn and misshapen. However, if there is no chest, copes can be stored on large wooden hangers which have been padded to minimize damage to the fabric. Traditionally, there were wooden chests made especially for copes and these can be seen in a few cathedrals and old churches. On very rare occasions, they are still made, but most churches would not be able to accommodate such a large and expensive piece of furniture.

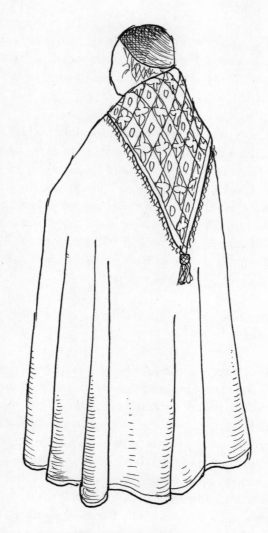

COPE (BACK)

Repair: as for other vestments, minor damage can usually be put right with careful hand-stitching, using good-quality thread of the appropriate colour and type. Other repairs need to be carried out professionally.

How worn: as a cloak over a cassock, alb and amice, cassock-alb, cassock with surplice or cotta, episcopal dress or other arrangements, but not over a chasuble, dalmatic or tunicle.

ACADEMIC HOOD
& SURPLICE

Scarf, academic hood and gown

Use: the scarf is worn by clergy and readers over a cassock and surplice, for conducting services and preaching, often with an academic hood. The hood can also be worn with a gown by, for example, church musicians.

Description: the scarf, also known as the tippet, is a broad band of cloth 18–25 centimetres (7–10 inches) wide and about 240 centimetres (8 feet) long. For clergy the scarf is usually black, and for readers usually blue. The ends may be pinked or straight and there are sometimes pleats or gathers at the neck. Cathedral clergy and chaplains to the Forces have badges sewn or embroidered on the ends of the scarf. Medals or medal ribbons can be worn on a scarf.

The hood is a narrow cape with a different-coloured facing, worn over the shoulders. The style, shape and colour depend on the university and type of degree.

The gown is a loose garment, usually open at the front, with gatherings at the back to form a yoke and with sleeves or split sleeves. The shape, colour and style of academic gowns depend on the university and type of degree. There are other types of gown. These include preaching, choir and Geneva gowns, which have fastenings at the front, and vergers' gowns.

Laundry: inexpensive scarves are often made of polyester and can be washed by hand or machine. The washing or

PREACHING GOWN

cleaning of other scarves depends on the fabric. Academic hoods should always be professionally dry-cleaned. Gowns can be made from a wide variety of materials, from polyester to silk, and care should be taken to wash or clean them appropriately.

Storage: scarves should be kept in a drawer. Academic hoods can be stored in a drawer or hung on a hook in a clean, dry place. Gowns should be kept on hangers of the appropriate size in a clean, dry place.

Repair: loose threads on scarves, hoods or gowns can be stitched by hand, using thread of the appropriate colour and type. More extensive damage, especially on hoods and gowns, needs to be dealt with professionally. Plain black or blue scarves, if badly torn, should ideally be replaced as a large repair would be visible on the plain background.

How worn: the scarf is worn around the neck over a cassock and surplice (or, in the case of bishops, over a rochet and chimere), with the ends of even length hanging down the front. The hood is worn over the shoulders, with the colours at the back, and secured at the front with a loop held in place by a button on the cassock. The hood is put on under the scarf. The gown is worn over a cassock or smart clothing.

ROCHET   CHIMERE

Rochet and chimere

Use: these are both episcopal vestments, worn by bishops for conducting usually non-eucharistic services and for other occasions, such as sitting in the House of Lords. In a slightly modified form, the chimere also has an academic use.

Description: the rochet is a full-length, white garment like a long surplice, made of fine linen, cotton or polycotton, usually with full sleeves gathered in at the wrist under black or red bands.

The chimere is a sleeveless gown, open at the front like an academic gown, with gathers between the shoulders at the back, now made usually of wool or a blend of wool and synthetic fibres, rather than silk or satin, as in the past. It is normally coloured red or black and the colour worn depends on the occasion. Traditionally, only those bishops who were Doctors of Divinity could wear the red chimere, but the distinction no longer applies. The wrist-bands match the colour of the chimere. The garment is thought to derive originally from a medieval riding coat.

Laundry: rochets can usually be washed and ironed, according to the method appropriate to the type of fabric used. Chimeres and matching wristbands normally need to be dry-cleaned.

ROCHET & CHIMERE

Storage: rochets and chimeres need to be kept on hangers, padded if appropriate, of the correct size, in a clean, dry place.

Repair: small tears or undone seams in rochets can be carefully mended by hand or machine using linen or cotton thread, as appropriate. Minor repairs to chimeres can be done by hand, using red or black thread of the appropriate type. More substantial repairs need to be done professionally.

How worn: the rochet is worn over a black or purple cassock and the chimere over the rochet, although when the bishop is also wearing a cope and mitre, the chimere is not normally worn. When worn as choir dress or habit, the rochet and chimere are worn with a black scarf or tippet, sometimes with academic hood, and white preaching bands.

According to the rubric of the *Book of Common Prayer* for the consecration of bishops, the bishop-elect wears cassock and rochet before the consecration and puts on the chimere (described as 'the rest of the Episcopal habit') immediately afterwards. This is still the case in England, but not in the whole of the Anglican Communion.

PREACHING BANDS

Bands, choir ruffs and collars

Use: these are all forms of white neckwear used, in the case of bands, by both clergy and laity, and, in the case of ruffs and collars, by choir members.

Description: bands are two strips of white linen, cotton, cotton muslin or polycotton, about 15 centimetres (6 inches) long, joined together. They are sometimes known as preaching bands. They often have tapes attached for tying at the back of the neck.

Choir ruffs and collars come in various styles.

Laundry: bands, if made of linen or cotton, are washed, starched and ironed with a moderately hot iron. If they are made of polycotton, they should be washed and then ironed with a cool iron.

Choir ruffs are washed and starched. If they are pleated, they need to be ironed carefully, with the pleats well pressed. If they are ruffled, they should be ironed so that the shape is maintained. If the fabric is polycotton rather than cotton, it should not be starched and ironing should be done with a cool iron.

Collars are washed, and also starched if they are of the stiff variety. All need to be ironed carefully.

Storage: in a drawer, compartment or box, labelled, in a clean, dry place.

CHOIR RUFF

Repair: small tears are probably best mended by hand, using linen or cotton thread.

How worn: bands can be worn with cassock, surplice and hood for the offices and other services or for preaching. They also form part of some academic or legal dress.

Choir ruffs and collars are worn by choir members, with cassocks or choir gowns.

Canterbury Cap

Mitre

Biretta

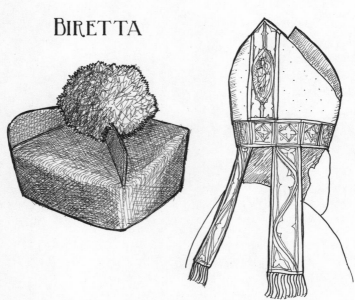

Mortarboard, Canterbury cap, biretta and mitre

Use: all are forms of ecclesiastical headwear, worn according to the occasion, parish tradition or individual preference. The mitre is worn only by bishops, although in the Middle Ages there were 'mitred abbots'. The mortarboard (also known as an academic cap or square), Canterbury cap and biretta are also worn in some academic and legal settings.

Description: the mortarboard, as its name suggests, features a flat, square board, usually black, covered in woollen or cotton cloth, attached to a skullcap-like section which fits on the top part of the head. It has a central tassel made of silk or another fabric.

The Canterbury cap is a square hat with sharp corners, made of woollen or a wool-mixture cloth, with four ridges on the top. It is soft and foldable. It is said to be the descendant of the Medieval cloth head-dress. It matches the colour of the cassock.

The biretta is a square, folding hat with three stiff ridges or horns and often a pom or tuft on top. It is usually made of black cloth with a silk pom.

The mitre is a tall folding cap, consisting of two similar parts (the front and back) rising in curves to a peak and sewn together at the sides. Two short lappets hang down from the back. It is made of a rich fabric, stiffened to hold the shape.

Laundry: all these forms of headwear require specialist cleaning.

Storage: all can be stored flat, in a drawer or box in a clean, dry place.

Repair: minor damage, such as an undone seam, can be stitched up carefully by hand, using appropriate thread. More substantial damage, especially to a mitre, needs a professional repair.

How worn: the mortarboard is worn horizontally on the head, with the tassel to one side, at the front. It is not worn in church, but may be carried.

The Canterbury cap, which can be worn by clergy or by female choir members, is worn diamond-shaped on the head, with a corner pointing forwards.

The biretta is worn with the ridge-less side on the left.

The mitre can be worn with a cope or chasuble, but not with choir dress.

Cleaning Church Textiles

Introduction to
Cleaning Church Textiles

Part Three provides more detail about washing, ironing and cleaning church textiles than on the previous pages. It includes a description of the most common fibres, both natural and synthetic, used in fabrics and gives guidance on types of washing product, dry-cleaning and stain removal.

None of the advice given is intended to be didactic, and users of the book will have their own reliable methods and good ideas. I have personally tried out numerous cleaning products and procedures over the years and have to admit to having had mixed success, especially over removing certain sorts of stains. Preventing stains in the first place is the ideal but, unfortunately, they seem to appear of their own accord.

Nearly all parishes need to be economical and there has to be a balance between this and the need to provide the cleanest, neatest and loveliest items for use in services. Most items of church linen and vestments will last for many years if they are looked after well, and repaired carefully when necessary. There is an elderly credence table cloth in my church which has, in the past, been meticulously mended using tiny squares of white linen, hand-sewn. When freshly washed and ironed, it still looks good and, when I look at those little squares, I think of the devotion of the unknown person who stitched them.

Checklist of fabrics

Natural fibres

Cotton

Cotton fabric is made using yarn or thread derived from the cotton plant, of the genus *gossypium*. The fibre, which is almost pure cellulose, comes from the fluffy ball that surrounds and protects the seeds. Cotton fabric has been used since antiquity in some parts of the world, but was not imported into Northern Europe until the late Medieval period. It is soft, breathable and comfortable to wear. Although generally off-white or pale brown in its natural state, it can be bleached white or dyed in almost any colour. It is also usually washable, absorbent and hard-wearing.

Linen

Linen is made from the fibres of the flax plant, *linum usitatissimum*. Like cotton, its use can be traced back to far antiquity. For example, the Egyptian mummies were wrapped in it. The fabric is smooth and cool to the touch, but gets softer with repeated washing. Although it is very durable and resists dirt and stains, constant creasing or ironing in the same place tends to break the threads. In its natural state, it is a pale, brownish colour, but it can be bleached white or dyed in any colour. One of its most noticeable characteristics is to crumple easily but, in some contexts, this is not seen as a disadvantage. Its use was widespread until the production of cheap cotton and 'linen' is still used as a general term for domestic goods such as bedding and towels or for underwear. The expression 'altar linen' is an example of such a usage.

Silk

Silk is made from a protein fibre obtained from the cocoons of insect larvae. Although there are wild silks that derive from a variety of caterpillars, most commercial silk is farmed using the cocoons of the larvae of the mulberry silkworm. Silk has many attractive properties. The fibre is triangular in cross-section, which means that the light is reflected from different angles, giving the fabric a shimmering shine. It is smooth, soft, durable and comfortable to wear. There are also disadvantages. Sunlight can weaken it and it can attract insects if stored badly. It also has poor elasticity and can shrink if washed. Dry-cleaning is advised for most silk items.

Wool

Wool is obtained from sheep and a few other animals, such as goats. The fleece that is removed from the sheep consists of clusters of wool fibres, known as staples. The length and thickness of the staples determine the ultimate use of the wool. Longer staples tend to be used to make worsted yarn, which is woven into cloth; shorter staples are used to make knitting wool. Wool is usually a creamy white in its natural state. Some types of wool can be hammered to make felt. In this process, the natural crimping of the fibres causes them to lock or hook together to form an unwoven cloth. Wool also contains grease, known as lanolin, and although this is mostly removed during processing – and put to other uses, such as hand cream – the small amount left in the wool helps to repel water. Wool is elastic and keeps its shape after washing or cleaning.

Synthetic fibres

Viscose

Viscose is a semi-synthetic fibre because although it is derived from wood pulp, chemicals are used in its manufacture. It was invented in the 1890s. The wood pulp is turned into sheets of cellulose and steeped in an alkali solution. After this, the sheets are shredded and treated with carbon disulphide and sodium hydroxide, making a thick, viscous solution – hence the name of the resulting fibre. The solution is forced through holes to regenerate the fibres, which are washed, dried, crimped and woven into fabric. The fabric is thought to be more like silk than cotton, and used to be known as artificial silk. It drapes well, can be dyed in any colour, and breathes like cotton. However, it tends to crumple and crease easily and it can shrink if washed in hot water. It also has poor elasticity, durability and insulating properties. Another common name for it is rayon.

Acetate

Acetate is very like viscose in being produced from wood pulp treated with chemicals. The fabric is soft and light-weight with a silky sheen. Its uses include linings for coats and jackets and the material for wedding dresses and ball gowns. It is comfortable to wear and does not retain moisture. It is usually dry-cleaned, although some acetate garments can be washed carefully, without wringing or stretching the fabric, as it has a tendency to crease when wet.

Nylon

Nylon is a synthetic polyamide, entirely man-made, and used in a wide variety of ways in addition to fabric. It was invented in the late 1930s in America, and an early and famous use was for women's stockings. The fabric has high elasticity and low absorption, which makes it suit-able for sportswear and swimsuits. It is strong, durable, easy to wash and usually requires no ironing, but is not particularly comfortable to wear apart from as sports clothing. A small amount of nylon is often mixed with other fibres to add strength to textiles used for clothing and furnishings.

Polyester

Polyesters are produced from chemical substances found mainly in petroleum and can be manufactured into textiles, packaging materials and many other products. Polyester fabric was first produced in the 1940s and became very popular over the next 30 to 40 years, being used for clothing, bedding and other items. It fell out of favour for a time after that, but superior polyester fibres and blends with natural fibres brought it back into fashion. The fabric has many advantages. It is inexpensive, strong, shrink-resistant, washable and quick-drying. On the minus side, it does not breathe and can be uncomfortable to wear. Furnishing fabrics made of polyester can have a 'cheap' appearance. Polyester is also not biodegradable. There are various brand names, including Terylene.

Mixtures

Polycotton

Polycotton is a mixture of cotton and polyester, often in the proportions 35 per cent cotton, 65 per cent polyester. When there is more cotton than polyester, some manufacturers describe the garments as 'cotton rich'. The fabric combines some of the advantages of both fibres, being crisp, cool, wrinkle-resistant and easy to wash and iron. However, it is not as breathable as cotton. It is widely used for clothing and bedding.

Cotton and viscose

Cotton is sometimes blended with viscose, in various proportions, to create a fabric that drapes more gracefully than pure cotton and has a slight sheen. It is usually washable.

Viscose and polyester

Fabric made of these two fibres combines the advantages of both, although still has some of the disadvantages. The viscose gives absorbency, softness, and the potential for a variety of colours. The polyester contributes durability and shape retention. The proportions are usually 35 per cent viscose and 65 per cent polyester.

Polyester and wool

This is a mixture often used for suiting. The polyester helps the garment to keep its shape and be durable while the wool provides warmth and absorbency. In general, the more polyester, the cheaper and less luxurious the cloth.

Terylene worsted

This is another version of the polyester and wool mixture. Wool is described as worsted when the fibres are combed and tightly twisted, so garments made from this fabric are very hard-wearing. For this reason, it is often used for school uniforms.

Wool and nylon

Nylon is sometimes added to wool, especially knitting wool, to give greater strength and durability. The proportions are typically 65 per cent wool, 35 per cent nylon.

Specialized fabrics

Brocade

Brocade is a patterned fabric woven on a shuttle loom. It is usually made of a rich fabric such as silk and the intricate design can have the effect of standing out from the background. It is used for furnishings and evening wear.

Jacquard

This is a weaving process invented by Joseph Marie Jacquard (1752–1834) in which a complex pattern can be produced mechanically. Brocades are usually woven using this process.

Damask

Named after the city of Damascus, which was a centre for its production in the Middle Ages, this fabric is woven in such a way that the pattern is slightly lustrous against a dull background. When the fabric is turned over, the shiny and dull areas are reversed. It is usually woven on Jacquard looms and can be made out of almost any fibre, natural or synthetic. It is often, although need not be, monochrome. It is used for table linen, furnishings and clothing.

Satin

This is a woven fabric with a smooth, glossy surface and a dull back. In order to produce the shiny top side, the yarn is woven so that most of the warp yarn lies on top of the weft yarn, rather than being fully integrated, as in other fabrics. Satin was traditionally always made of silk and regarded as a very luxurious material. However, it can now be made of synthetic fibres such as polyester and nylon. It is used for underwear, bedding and furnishings.

Velvet

This is a woven fabric which has an evenly cut, tufted surface. Originally made from silk, it was regarded as a luxury material before modern processes and synthetic fibres came into use. It can be made from most sorts of natural and synthetic fibre, but silk velvet is still the softest and most expensive. It can be used for a wide range of furnishings and clothing. Generally, it needs to be dry-cleaned.

Hopsack

This is a loosely or coarsely woven material where the criss-cross pattern of the weaving resembles sacking or basketwork. It has a more rustic look than a tightly woven fabric. Although it was originally produced using wool, cotton or linen, it can now be made from synthetic fibres, principally polyester.

What to wash and what not to wash

What to wash

The following items can usually be washed safely, but see the individual entries to check on machine- and hand-washing. When in doubt over how to wash a delicate item, choose hand-washing.

1 Anything that is washable according to the label.
2 Linen or cotton items, including purificators, corporals, palls, lavabo towels, surplices, cottas, albs and altar cloths.
3 Items made of mixtures of cotton, linen, viscose or polyester, including surplices and cottas.
4 Polyester items, including cassocks, cassock-albs and choir gowns.
5 When appropriate, lace and embroidered cotton, provided they are carefully hand-washed in lukewarm water, without twisting or wringing.

What not to wash

The following items usually need to be dry-cleaned, with specialist advice if necessary.

1 Anything that is labelled 'Dry-clean only'.
2 Vestments, including chasubles, copes, dalmatics, tunicles, maniples and stoles, unless it is certain that they are washable.
3 Items made of woollen cloth, or a wool blend, including cassocks and cassock-albs, unless the label says that the item is washable.
4 Silk chalice veils and the outer coverings of burses.
5 Altar frontals and palls, and pulpit and lectern falls, unless they are known to be washable.
6 Old or delicate embroidered fabric of any type when hand-washing is not appropriate.
7 Items made of velvet, whether cotton velvet or silk velvet.

Laundering, dry-cleaning and stain removal

Laundering

Soap

Although the terms 'soap' and 'detergent' are often used interchangeably, the two products are different. Soap, which has been manufactured for thousands of years, is a salt of a fatty acid, produced by treating vegetable or animal oils with a strongly alkaline solution, usually sodium hydroxide or potassium hydroxide. Historically, soap was made with mutton fat and the burnt ashes of bracken or other plants (potash). The chemical reaction that produces soap is known as saponification, from the Latin word *sapo*, for soap. Soap works as an emulsifying agent, allowing insoluble particles – for example, fats, with dirt sticking to them – to become soluble in water and rinsed away. The disadvantage is that in hard water, insoluble salts are formed, often referred to as scum or a tide mark.

Detergents

During the First World War, when animal and vegetable fat was needed for other purposes, synthetic detergents began to be developed. It was not until after the Second World War, however, that detergents for domestic laundry became widely available. They are chemical compounds which, like soap, act as surfactants, lowering the surface tension between two liquids or between a liquid and a solid. The word 'surfactant' is a short form of 'surface active agent'. Detergents have an advantage over soap in that they are fully soluble in hard water without forming scum. Branded washing detergents, in both powdered and liquid form, contain a number of ingredients apart from surfactants, including water softeners, bleaches, brighteners and perfume.

Biological detergents

Since the 1970s, biological laundry detergents have been available and many washing powders, liquids and gels on the supermarket shelves are now of this type. These contain enzymes that have been gathered from micro-organisms. They break down fats, starches and proteins and are therefore effective in removing stains caused by, for example, food, mud or perspiration. They are bio-degradable and work best at lower temperatures, which is good for the environment. However, there are a few disadvantages. It is thought by some users that they cause skin irritation, although others dispute this. There is probably more evidence that, used over a long period, biological detergents can cause colours to fade, especially those derived from vegetable dyes. This is an important point to consider in connection with the washing of church textiles.

Environmentally friendly washing powders and liquids

Although surfactants of one sort or another are essential for getting dirt out of fabrics, most of those used in washing powders and liquids are not naturally occurring. This would not be a problem if they were all biodegradable, but, unfortunately, many are not. Phosphates are another questionable ingredient of many detergents. Phosphates help the cleaning process, especially in hard water, but, when released into waterways, can endanger fish and other aquatic life.

Because of these concerns, manufacturers have developed 'eco' cleaning products, using plant-based surfactants as opposed to petrochemical-based ones. Although these seem clearly to be preferable, there are other factors to be considered. For example, some users believe that they do not clean so effectively as the soap or detergent-based cleaning products available and either use more of the product or wash the items more frequently. This leads to a greater use of water and energy, including through manufacturing and transportation, which, again, can hurt the environment. It is best to research the arguments before coming to any firm conclusion over which washing agent to use.

Machine- and hand-washing

Most washable items can be washed safely in the washing-machine, using the manufacturer's guidelines as to timing and temperature, although check for labels that say 'Hand-wash only'. Hand-washing is appropriate, even essential, for lace, embroidered and delicate items, especially if they are old, provided they can be safely washed at all. Old lace can usually be washed very gently by hand, using several changes of warm water, but it should never be twisted or wrung out. A gentle washing liquid is best, either a soap liquid or a mild detergent. Linen and cotton, if not delicate or embroidered, can be boiled. For machine-washing, the choice of washing powder, soap flakes or liquid is a matter for personal preference and it is good to experiment until the favourite emerges. Soaking items in bleach before washing them is not at all advisable because bleach weakens the fabric and will shorten its life.

It is worth remembering, also, that items of church linen or vestments do not always have care labels on them. When there is no label, particular care should be taken to identify the fabric and choose the most appropriate cleaning method, using this guide.

Dry-cleaning

Dry-cleaning is cleaning without water, but it is not really dry, as the item is immersed in a liquid solvent, usually percholoroethylene. It is suitable for fabrics that shrink, stretch, become floppy or are otherwise damaged by washing in water, although some decorative trims are not compatible with solvents, either. It should never be assumed, therefore, that if an item is unsuitable for washing, it is suitable for dry-cleaning. If there is any doubt, professional dry-cleaning staff should be consulted.

When an item has been delivered to the dry-cleaning shop, it is first inspected for stains or marks, and these are treated with a specialist stain-remover. After this, it is placed with other similar articles in a dry-cleaning machine and put through a cleaning cycle. The machine contains a tank for the solvent, a pump, a filter and a cylinder. The solvent is pumped through the filter into the cylinder which holds the items and flushes through them before returning to the tank via a trap. This process is repeated an appropriate number of times. After this, the solvent is drained from the cylinder and an extractor cycle is run to draw all the solvent out of the items. Warm air is then circulated through the cylinder to vaporize any remaining solvent. The vapour is collected and condensed back to a liquid before being pumped back into the tank. Finally, the items are removed from the machine, finished and pressed, as necessary, and hung up.

There are products on the market that are for 'dry-cleaning' at home, using a tumble dryer or washer/dryer (on the 'dryer' setting). Typically, these contain perfume plus chemicals such as methylchloroisothiazolinone and methylisothiazolinone. The chemicals have antibacterial and antifungal properties and are used in a wide range of skin-care products, including wet-wipes. However, they can also be irritants or cause allergic reactions. The instructions (which should always be read carefully) usually advise treating spots and fresh stains on the fabric first, using the 'wipe' provided, and then placing the garment in the dryer with the 'wipe' for about 20 minutes on a low heat. The latter process does not clean the item, but 'refreshes' it by infusing it with perfume (which may not be to everybody's liking). As these products have limited cleaning properties and cannot, in any case, be used on silk, velvet and various other materials, they are not appropriate for most church textiles.

Stain removal

Stains are almost unavoidable, however much care is taken, but they are a nuisance. Stains on communion linen are most likely to be of wine, soot or lipstick. Those on surplices, cottas, albs, cassocks and eucharistic vestments are often of candle wax. Flower pollen can get on to linen and garments. Wine and wax can also get on to carpets and furnishings. All can be difficult to remove.

In some cases, the following advice mentions forms of alcohol. Alcohol includes surgical spirit and methylated spirits. Both of these are composed mainly of ethanol and both are volatile and flammable. Neither should ever be drunk. *Alcohol, including surgical spirit and methylated spirits, should be handled with the utmost care and kept away from children and vulnerable adults.*

Some common stains and how to tackle them

Wine

Wine stains may present particularly sensitive issues. In denominations, parishes or congregations where Transubstantiation, Metousiosis or the concept of the Real Presence is a part of the doctrine or prevailing view, stains formed from wine that has been consecrated should be dealt with only in the traditional way. This indicates that the stains can be rinsed through or soaked in clean, fresh water only (no soap, detergent or cleaning agent should be used), with the water being subsequently disposed of by being poured away on to soil (the 'good earth') with due reverence. Should this fail adequately to remove the stains, no further cleaning (other than repeating the process) should take place, and the appropriate course of action is then to destroy the vestment, garment or linen item by burning. In circumstances where these beliefs and views do not apply, wine stains can be treated with a proprietary stain-remover, following the manufacturer's instructions. Bleach, such as diluted hydrogen peroxide, is not recommended because it ultimately weakens the fabric.

Lipstick

Lipstick is oil-based, so the cleaning agent should be something that will tackle grease. There are proprietary stain-removers which deal with lipstick stains. Otherwise, if the stain is on cotton or linen, it should first be dabbed carefully with a swab dipped in alcohol, then treated with a drop of liquid detergent or powdered detergent made into a paste with water. Finally, the item should be laundered in the usual way. If the item is normally dry-cleaned, it should not be placed in water or washed, but can be dabbed carefully with alcohol. Precious or delicate items should be professionally cleaned.

Wax

The traditional way to remove wax is first to let it set (possibly in the refrigerator), then to scrape off any raised areas with a blunt knife or plastic card and finally to apply a moderately hot iron over brown, blotting or kitchen paper, with the stained fabric under it and another piece of paper between the item and the ironing board. Cotton or linen can be put in a hot wash after this. Polycotton or synthetic items should be washed at a lower temperature. On items such as polycotton surplices and cottas, these methods can be only partially successful and the remaining wax can get 'set' in the fabric. Both wax and synthetic fibres are resistant to water, so washing the item subsequently does not make much difference. Items that are normally dry-cleaned should not be placed in water. The mark should be shown to the dry-cleaning staff when the item is taken to be cleaned.

Soot

Soot from candles is very unsightly on white linen and, as it often has wax mixed in with it, is very difficult to remove. The first thing to do is to try brushing off any loose soot, very gently, with a soft paintbrush or tooth-brush. If the soot still looks fairly loose but has not all come off, try covering the mark with baking powder, leaving it for an hour or so, and brushing it again. Next, inspect the mark for traces of wax. If there are any, use the suggestions listed under 'wax'. If there appears to be no wax but the soot has still not come off, moisten a cotton handkerchief with alcohol, place the cloth on a board with a piece of kitchen paper under it, and dab the mark carefully with the handkerchief. With luck, this will remove more of the soot. Finally, linen, cotton or syn-thetic items will need to be washed carefully, following the normal washing instructions. Items that are normally dry-cleaned should not be washed. As with all stained fabrics, the stain should be shown to the staff at the dry-cleaning shop.

Flower pollen

Like soot, pollen can produce a very noticeable stain. One of the loveliest flowers, and one often used in church flower arrangements, the lily, makes the worst marks. Not only does the pollen fall on to the surface below the arrangement, it has a nasty habit of getting on to people's clothing when they pass too close, especially on surplices and cottas.

The first thing to do is to shake the fabric and, if you are fortunate, the pollen will come off. At this stage, it should not be touched with the fingers, as the oil in skin can cause the mark to 'set'. Similarly, it should not be dabbed with water, as this will dissolve the particles and make the problem worse. If shaking the item has not removed all of the pollen, place sticky tape over the mark and pull it off gently. This can be repeated several times. If, after this, a stain lingers, more radical action is needed. If the item is washable, it should be soaked in cold water for an hour or two and then washed in the usual way. The stain can be rubbed lightly with washing liquid or powder before the item is washed. Items that are normally dry-cleaned should not be placed in water. When they are taken to be dry-cleaned, the stain should be identified.

Spills on a carpet

Wine or wax spilt on the church carpet can be tackled as follows:

Wine

Again, the approach will need to reflect the doctrine or local prevailing view when consecrated wine has been spilt. Where a belief in Transubstantiation, Metousiosis or 'Real Presence' applies, the carpet should be treated with clean, fresh water only (in the same way as is specified for vestments and linens, above) and the situation should otherwise be handled in exactly the same way as for vestments and linens. If these particular views and beliefs do not apply, or if the spillage is unconsecrated wine, the wine can be blotted with an absorbent rag or kitchen paper as soon as possible or, if this is unrealistic, covered with salt and tackled later. When no more wine can be soaked up, clean the area carefully with a cloth or sponge dipped in soapy water or a very mild detergent. Alternatively, try mixing one-third white vinegar with two-thirds cold or lukewarm water and dab gently. Finish by dabbing with clean water.

(Where consecrated wine has been mopped up, the kitchen paper or rag should properly be dried and reverently disposed of safely and privately.)

Wax

Leave to harden, then scrape off carefully. Any remains can be covered with a clean absorbent rag or brown paper and ironed carefully with a warm iron. If any stain remains, a small amount of methylated spirits on a rag can be rubbed very gently over the mark.

Starching and ironing

Starching

Starch is a carbohydrate derived from cereals and it is used to add stiffness to certain materials to prevent them from creasing and getting dirty easily. Some items of church linen definitely need to be starched if they are to look their best and handle well. Other items should not be starched and can look quite comical if they are. For example, a stiffly starched surplice can end up looking like a bell tent. Items of church linen that are used to soak up water – for example, lavabo towels – should never be starched because the starch inhibits absorption.

In this guide, where each item is described, a note about starching, or not starching, is included.

Although spray starches are quick and easy to use, the best results are obtained from traditional powdered or liquid starch. If this cannot be found in the local shops, suppliers can be located online. The starching instructions supplied with the product should be followed.

Ironing

Items made of linen or cotton, or a mixture of the two, should ideally be ironed with a steam iron, usually on a fairly hot setting. Both are best ironed while they are still damp and not damped after becoming dry. This is particularly the case with linen, as it is harder to remove ugly creases once the fabric has completely dried. If only a dry iron is available, good results can be obtained by spraying water on the item first.

Items of altar linen generally need to be folded and ironed in a particular way. This is described on the entry for each item.

If an item is embroidered – as are some altar cloths, corporals, lavabo towels, palls and purificators – it should first be ironed carefully face up and then from the back so as to 'raise' the embroidery. Care should be taken not to iron over the embroidery again when the item is being folded. It is important to check the composition of the embroidery thread before the item is ironed, in case it requires special attention. It is sometimes a good idea to cover the embroidery with a clean, old cotton handkerchief while it is being ironed, in order to protect it.

Items made of polycotton, such as surplices and cottas, do not necessarily need to be ironed, especially if they have been left to drip dry, but they usually look better if a very moderate iron has been put over them. It is important that the iron is not hot because the synthetic constituent of the fabric scorches and even melts under heat.

Items made entirely of polyester, such as cassocks and choir robes, should not be ironed, except with a very cool iron.

PART FOUR

Storage, Disposal and Acquisition

Introduction to Storage, Disposal and Acquisition

This section gives guidance on the storage of textiles and on how to assess whether to dispose of items or acquire new ones. Diocesan Advisory Committees (DACs) often produce their own advice leaflets or will gladly answer individual queries. Most DACs have at least one member who is an expert on church textiles and this expertise is available to parishes. Trying to decide what to do over a well-loved but shabby item is not easy, even for the most experienced and knowledgeable clergy and laity, and there is no shame over seeking help.

Those of us who look after vestries or sacristies would love to have clean, dry, spacious rooms, complete with shining cupboards, chests and drawers, all bearing clear and accurate labels. Although such vestries do no doubt exist, the reality for most of us is very different. Some vestries are dark or cramped, with bulging racks full of rarely washed cassocks, cottas or other garments; some are curtained-off parts of medieval churches where there is one old cupboard and a set of shelves, all looking slightly dusty when sunshine filters through a stained-glass window; others are business-like enough in appearance but hideously overcrowded because nobody has ever disposed of anything.

Bringing a greater sense of order to a vestry or sacristy need not be expensive. Labelling boxes and drawers, introducing a laundering system, keeping clear records and attending to areas of damp will all improve matters without very much expenditure. A well-run vestry will both help to conserve textiles and support the parish's ministry and mission.

Storage

Keeping records and making labels

Every parish should maintain an inventory of the contents of the church, updated as necessary and checked annually, if possible. In the case of vestments and hangings, a brief description should be included, noting the date of the item, if known, and the designer or supplier. It is also a good idea to include photographs in order to assist with identification.

Small linen items, such as purificators and lavabo towels, do not always find their way into church inventories, but it is still good practice to maintain a list of them. This can also include basic information about their condition so that a watch is kept on the need for repairs and so that new purchases can be included in parish budgets.

However items are stored – whether in cupboards, drawers, boxes or chests – labelling is essential. It is so much more convenient to be able to locate an item quickly and accurately than to search through drawers and cupboards looking for it while rapidly losing one's composure. It is also kinder to new volunteers or staff members to introduce them to a tidy vestry where everything is labelled than to an ecclesiastical representation of chaos. It is important, also, to keep the labelling up to date and to make sure that the label still describes what is contained in the receptacle.

The best conditions for storage

Most churches do not have the best conditions for storage but can usually make adjustments in order to provide the best conditions possible. It is important to know how textiles are affected by the environment in which they are kept. Once there is an awareness of the effects of everyday conditions, such as light and heat, the task of looking after church textiles becomes more routine and intelligible. The most common problems are listed below.

Dust

Dust is everywhere and churches that are in normal use cannot escape their share. Dust contains a wide range of tiny particles, including flower pollen, human skin cells, hairs, fibres from clothing and paper, and soil. However, there are simple steps that can be taken in order to protect church linen, hangings and vestments from the worst effects of dust. These include keeping items in their proper places when not in use, making sure that cupboard doors are kept closed, covering up stored frontals with dust covers if they are not in special chests, and not leaving used items of linen lying around.

Light

Sunlight can cause irreversible damage to textiles, causing colours to fade and fibres to become weak and brittle. Some forms of lighting, such as bright spotlights, can also cause damage, especially if heat is generated. In the areas where textiles are in use, for example in chancels, a few minor adjustments can make a great deal of difference and possibly add years to the life of a particular item. It may be possible to change the lighting, either by altering the position of the fittings or by replacing the bulbs with ones that have less impact. In some buildings, blinds or curtains can be introduced in order to prevent strong sunlight from falling constantly on coloured textiles.

In the areas where textiles are stored, items can be fully protected by being kept in chests, cupboards or drawers, or by having cloth covers placed over them.

Extremes of temperature

Textiles do not fare well when the atmosphere is either too hot or too cold. However, in a typical parish, where there is little spare money for providing optimal levels of heating all the year round, it can be very difficult to ensure the best temperature for textiles. At certain times of the year, in spring and autumn, when the church heating is either not turned on or is at a low setting, the temperature is about right. But, in the middle of summer or in the depths of winter, the temperature is likely to be too high or too low. Even so, there are adjustments that can be made and cost little or nothing. Vestments should never be hung over hot radiators or kept in a sunny corner of the vestry. Similarly, they should be kept away from cold draughts.

Humidity

A warm, damp atmosphere can be detrimental to church textiles because it provides the ideal conditions for mould and mildew to take hold. Also, if there is a lack of ventilation, condensation occurs when there is a drop in temperature. Churches in some parts of the country have perennial problems with dampness because of the prevailing weather conditions, and parish officers may feel that there is little that they can do. There is, however, much that can be done to alleviate the situation. Ventilation in cupboards can be improved by drilling holes in doors or fitting grilles. Textiles can be hung well away from damp walls or spacers can be fixed between walls and the racks where garments or vestments are hung in order to ensure that the fabrics do not touch the walls. It is also important to keep the hems of items a few centimetres above the floor, because fabric will soak up moisture from a damp floor.

Pests

It does not need much imagination to realize that rats, mice and insects such as moths can do permanent damage to textiles or ruin them completely. The best ways to prevent such damage are to keep vestries and other areas clean and tidy, to make sure that food and sweet drinks are not left lying about, to recognize the signs of an invasion (such as mouse droppings and moth-holes), and to carry out regular checks. When the visitors or residents are bats, however, neither the creatures nor their roosts should be touched, because bats are a protected species. When a parish is planning building work that is likely to affect the bats, advice should be sought from the DAC at an early stage.

Methods of storage

Flat storage

This includes storage in chests, drawers or boxes. As a general rule, items should be folded as little as possible and, where they have to be folded, acid-free tissue paper inserted in the folds will help to prevent creases and extend the life of the fabric. The container should not be overcrowded and care should be taken to close the lids or drawers fully in order to prevent edges of fabric being trapped or left hanging out. Polythene should never be used for storage because it attracts dirt and does not let the fabrics breathe.

There are some reliable and inexpensive methods for storing delicate fabrics and embroidered items. Cardboard tubes, on which things like kitchen foil are rolled, make excellent bases for items that should not be folded. The item is rolled carefully round the tube, interleaving with acid-free tissue paper, and if there is embroidery, this should be on the outside. Clean, old cotton sheets can be cut up and stitched to form washable linings for drawers and covers for rolled-up items.

If the parish uses vestments in liturgical colours, a chest with a number of drawers is the ideal receptacle, because there can be a drawer for each colour and possibly a spare drawer where linen, in labelled compartments, can be stored. This need not be a specially made vestment chest. Inexpensive plan chests, with wide drawers and convenient holders for labels, can be obtained, new or secondhand, from office furniture suppliers.

Hanging storage

Most vestries have an area where items are hung up, in a cupboard, on a rack or in a special frontal chest. Routine garments, such as cassocks, surplices and choir gowns, are nearly always stored hanging from a rail. These do not require special hangers but the hangers should be of the correct size, be made of wood, apart from the hook, and have a hook that is long enough not to rub the collar of the garment. In the most ordered vestries, the items are hung according to some system, such as size or category. Wire hangers, of the sort provided by dry-cleaning shops, should never be used in vestries.

When vestments are hung up rather than being stored in chests, special considerations apply, apart from those relating to temperature, lighting and so on. Chasubles, dalmatics and tunicles need sturdy hangers of the right size, with the arms long enough not to poke through the fabric, and ideally padded in order to prevent wear and tear. They should not be crowded or squashed together. Copes can be hung along the middle of the back over a padded roller. In vestries where drawer space is available but limited, it is a good idea to hang up the items that are in current use and to keep the others in drawers, changing them round as required. In parishes where 'sets' of vestments are used only occasionally, the provision of an extra chasuble will help to conserve the one that belongs with the set. This is rather like buying a suit with two pairs of trousers.

Heavy items, especially altar frontals and falls, are never easy to store. If they are stored in flat chests or drawers, great care needs to be taken over preventing creasing. If they are stored hanging, in cupboards or special chests, they need to be hung on stout, padded rollers that are well supported at each end. If funds are limited, suitable rollers can often be obtained, free of charge, from carpet shops that wish to dispose of the rollers used for carpeting and rugs. These, when cut to size and padded, make very acceptable storage rollers.

Disposal and acquisition

Disposal

Every parish has its own needs, aims and traditions, so there can be no general rule about disposing of items of church linen or vestments. When these are cared for sensibly and lovingly, and stored in good conditions, they will last for a very long time. Some parishes are still joyfully using items that are over a century old. But none of these items will last for ever. The day comes when disposal becomes a possibility or necessity.

In the case of linen, a good deal of careful laundering, mending and stain-removal will have taken place before somebody dares suggest that the item has reached the end of its useful life. Then it should be disposed of sensitively. Sometimes, however, a gift of new linen is received before the existing linen really needs to be replaced. In that situation, tactful enquiries might be made of neighbouring parishes to see if the current stock can be donated to a parish that could make good use of it.

In the case of eucharistic vestments, much more consideration is needed before a decision is made about disposal.

If the items are historic or beautifully decorated, the DAC should be asked for advice. Embroidered decoration can often be 'lifted' from worn-out background material and remounted on new material, sometimes to beautiful effect. When the items are still in good condition but the parish does not wish to use them in its worship any more, they need not necessarily be disposed of but, instead, stored for possible future use. Customs change and go in cycles. If that is not practicable because of lack of storage space, enquiries should be made to find out if another parish would be able to use the items. Throwing vestments away is a last resort.

Acquisition

There are occasions when a parish will want to acquire new or different items of linen, garments or vestments. In the case of linen and garments, there are several suppliers, both at home and abroad, that offer a wide range of products. They nearly always have their own websites and will gladly offer advice. The old saying about getting what you pay for is probably right and the practical approach is to choose the best quality for the available funds.

In the case of vestments, much more research and discussion is needed before a decision can be made. If another parish is offering its cast-offs, there is no need to accept them unless they can be used and liked. When a purchase is to be made, there are several questions that require answers. What is the budget? What colour and fabric are required? Is the item to be for 'everyday' use or for special occasions? Is it to be bought off-the-peg or custom-made? How much decoration is appropriate? Is there a favourite designer or embroiderer?

Plenty of advice is available. The DAC can be consulted. Local parishes that have recently purchased vestments will not mind displaying them and describing the considerations that influenced them in choosing those particular items. Suppliers are always glad to answer questions, offer advice, and provide swatches of materials. Only when all the questions have been answered should the purchase be made.

All in all, it is a privilege to use and care for church linen and vestments. Choosing washing powders, removing stains and labelling drawers may not seem to be the most glamorous – or devout – activities, but they all play their part in ensuring that the textiles that are handled or worn in church are in the best condition possible.

Appendix:
The Liturgical Colours

In many parishes, the seasons of the Christian Year are marked by the appropriate liturgical colour for vestments, altar frontal, pulpit fall and so on. Most lectionaries and church calendars include a note about the relevant liturgical colour, but it helps to know the symbolic meaning and the pattern of use. Although *Common Worship* gives guidance on the appropriate colours, there are wide variations in tradition among individual parishes. For example, unbleached linen is used by some churches during Lent and there are distinctions between gold and white in parishes that possess vestments in both colours. Where a parish has both gold and white vestments, the gold ones are generally kept for the most important seasons, such as Easter and Christmas.

Similarly, there are some days in the year when parishes may be faced with either continuing a long-standing practice or moving to a practice suggested by *Common Worship*. An example would be using red instead of green for the last four Sundays of the liturgical year (the Kingdom Season), or white for the whole 'new' Epiphany season up until Candlemas. *Common Worship* also suggests red for the Monday, Tuesday and Wednesday of Holy Week.

Many parishes store their coloured vestments in special vestment chests, using each drawer for a specific colour.

The guidance below is not intended to be either dogmatic or definitive. The main colours are:

PURPLE OR VIOLET: used to symbolize penitence and preparation and suitable for:
Advent (although a few churches use blue)
Lent (although some churches have special unbleached linen Lenten and red Passiontide hangings)
Vigils
Rogation days
Services of Requiem

ROSE PINK: used to symbolize joy and happiness and suitable for:
Third Sunday in Advent (also known as Gaudete Sunday)
Fourth Sunday in Lent (Mothering Sunday or Laetare Sunday)

WHITE, CREAM OR GOLD: used to symbolize glory, purity or joy and suitable for:
Christmas
Epiphany

Candlemas (Presentation of Christ in the Temple)
Easter
Ascension
Trinity Sunday
Festivals of the Blessed Virgin Mary
Michaelmas
All Saints' Day
Corpus Christi
The Transfiguration
Saints who were not martyred

GREEN: used to symbolize growth and hope and suitable
for:
Trinitytide Sundays (after Trinity Sunday)
All 'ordinary' or 'ferial' days of the year

RED: used to symbolize fire and blood and suitable for:
The Kingdom Season (the period between All Saints and
Advent)
Palm Sunday and Good Friday
Monday, Tuesday and Wednesday of Holy Week
Pentecost/Whitsunday
Martyrs

BLACK: used to symbolize death and mourning and
suitable for:
All Souls' Day
Services of Requiem
Good Friday (in some traditions)
Funerals